Dear Reader,

When Susy Clemens began writing a biography of her famous father, she kept it a secret—and hid the notebook under her pillow. But YOU get to read it. All the entries on the notebook pages inside are from Susy's secret biography. I hope you enjoy getting to know the extraordinary Mark Twain (according to Susy)!

Barbara Kerley

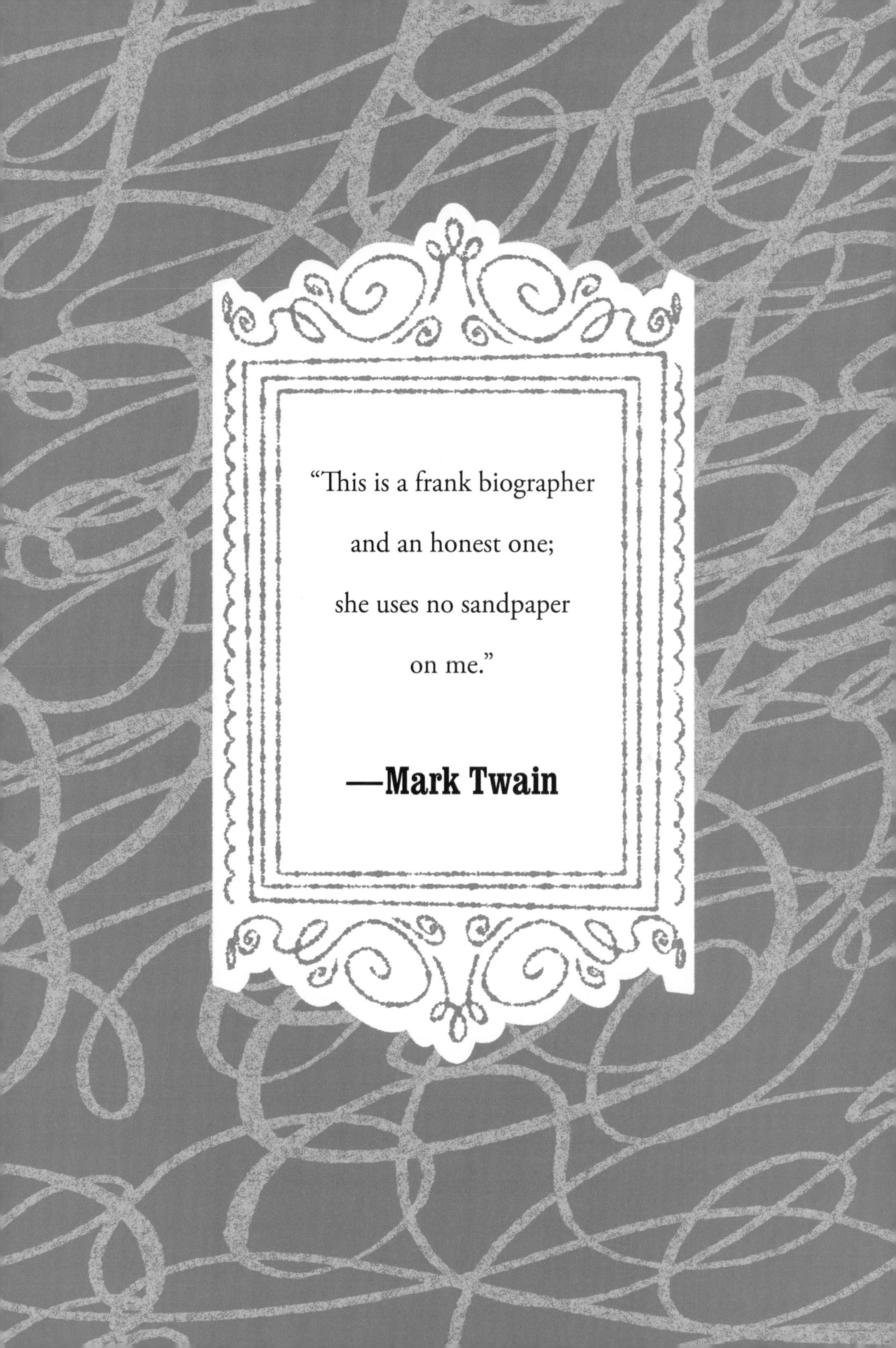

“This is a frank biographer
and an honest one;
she uses no sandpaper
on me.”

—Mark Twain

The Extraordinary
Mark Twain
(According to Susy)

By **Barbara KERLEY**

Illustrated by
Edwin FOTHERINGHAM

SCHOLASTIC INC.
New York Toronto London Auckland
Sydney New Delhi Hong Kong

According to Susy,
people were . . . well,
just plain wrong
about her papa.

They *thought* they knew Mark Twain — after all, he was a world-famous author, quoted here, there, and everywhere. Thousands of people had read his books and attended his lectures.

People probably thought they were Mark Twain *experts*.

But they were wrong, and Susy was "**annoyed.**" Greatly.

"It troubles me to have so few people know Papa, I mean really know him," Susy said. **"They think of Mark Twain as a humorist, joking at everything."**

Mark Twain *was* a humorist. Some folks called him the funniest man in America. But he was more — so much more. **"I never saw a man with so much variety of feeling as Papa has,"** Susy said, and she was determined to set the record straight.

Susy was thirteen. Papa called her **"the busiest bee in the household hive,"** but he didn't realize just how busy: Susy was secretly writing her *own* biography of Mark Twain.

We are a very happy family! we consist of papa, mamma, Jean Clara and me. It is papa I am writing about, and I shall have no trouble in not knowing what to say about him, as he is a very striking character. Papa's appearance has been discribed many times, but very incorectly; he has beautiful curly grey hair, not any

too thick, or any too long, just right;
A roman nose, which greatly improves
the beauty of his features, kind blue
eyes, and a small mustache . . . in
short he is an extrodinarily fine looking
man. All his features are perfect exept
that he hasn't extrodinary teeth.

Susy Clemens.
Farmington Ave.
Hartford Ct.

To write a good biography, Susy knew she must capture her subject's personality: his character quirks and the little things that made Papa, well . . . Papa.

She studied him by day . . . and wrote about him at night. Then she hid the biography under her pillow.

Susy observed Papa carefully — how he stopped whatever he was doing, just to confer with a cat; how he paced the floor between courses at dinner, waving his napkin to punctuate a particular point; and how he let the housekeeper know when his shirts were missing buttons.

Susy noted Papa's habits. She described his fine qualities. She even described his not-so-fine qualities. Into the biography — and under the pillow — it all went.

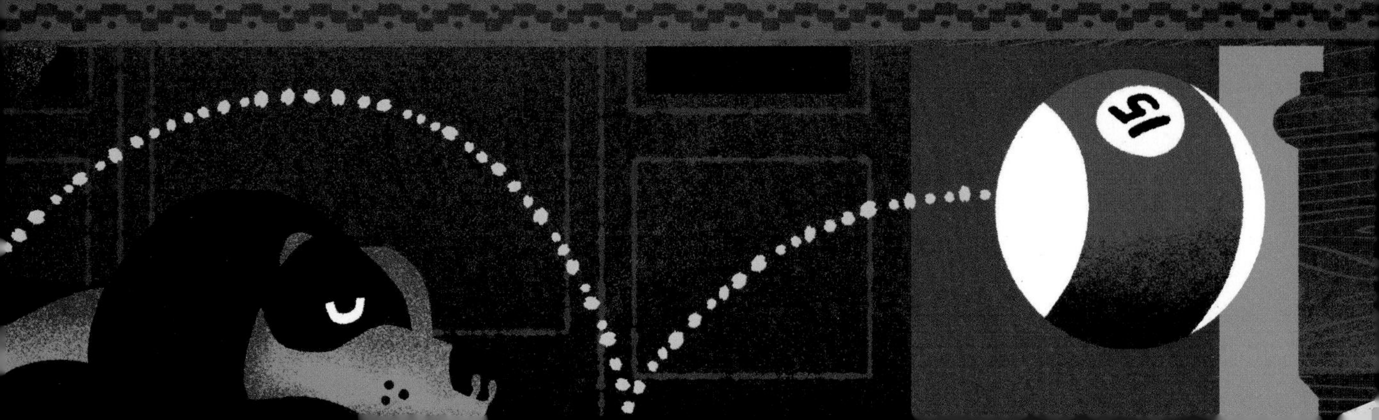

He does tell perfectly delightful stories. . . .

He has a peculiar gait we like, it seems just to sute him . . . he always walks up and down the room while thinking. . . .

His favorite game is billiards, and when he is tired, . . . he stays up all night and plays . . . it seems to rest his head. . . .

He has got a temper but we all of us have in this family. . . .

He is . . . oh so absent minded! . . .

He smokes a great deal almost incessantly. . . .

Papa uses very strong language.

One day, Mamma found the biography and showed it to Papa.

He examined the book with **"deep pleasure,"** delighting in Susy's **"frequently desperate"** spelling. He approved of how she didn't **"cover up one's deficiencies but gave them an equal showing with one's handsomer qualities."**

But most of all, Papa was touched that Susy had started the biography **"secretly and of her own motion and out of love"** for him.

It was the finest compliment he had ever received.

After that, Papa sometimes made pronouncements about himself at the breakfast table just to help his biographer along. And if his biographer needed to fill in the blanks, she just asked.

Papa said the other day, "I am a mugwump and a mugwump is pure from the marrow out." (Papa knows that I am writing this biography of him, and he said this for it.) He doesn't like to go to church at all, why I never understood, until just now, he told me the other

day, that he couldn't bear to hear
any one talk but himself, but that
he could listen to himself talk for
hours without getting tired, of course
he said this in joke, but I've no
dought it was founded on truth.

Like any good biographer, Susy chronicled Papa's early years.

HANNIBAL

Papa was born in Misouri. . .

And we know papa played "Hookey" all the time and how readily would papa have pretended to be dying so as not to have to go to school!

Grandma couldn't make papa go to school, so she let him go into a printing office to learn the trade. He did so, and gradually picked up enough education to enable him to do

about as well as those who were more
studious in early life. He was about
20 years old when he went on the
Mississippi as a pilot. . . . then he
reported for a newspaper, and was
on several newspapers; then he was
sent to the Sandwich Islands. . . .
After that he came back to America
and his friends wanted him to lecture,
so he lectured.

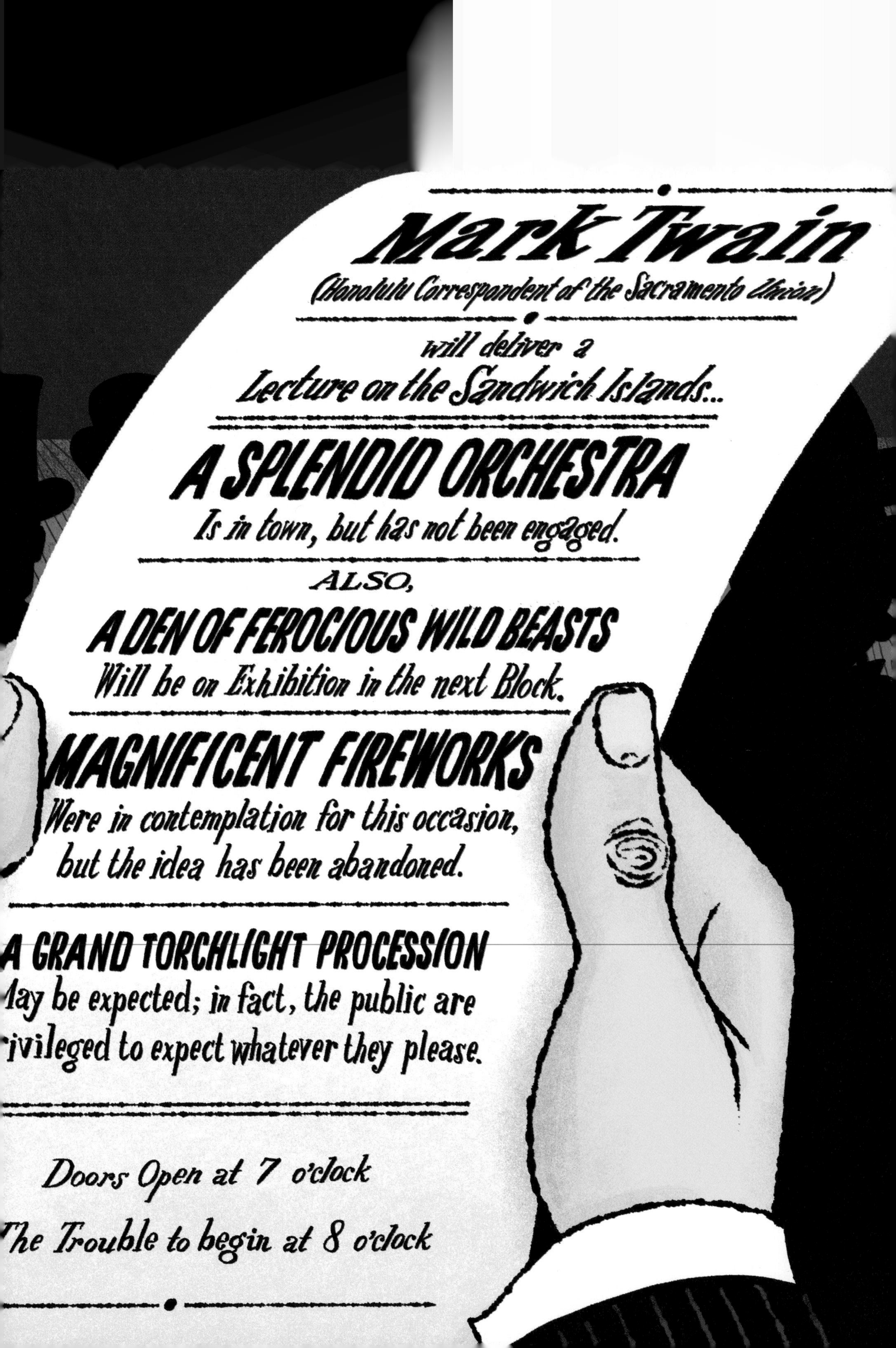
Mark Twain
(Honolulu Correspondent of the Sacramento Union)
will deliver a
Lecture on the Sandwich Islands...
A SPLENDID ORCHESTRA
Is in town, but has not been engaged.
ALSO,
A DEN OF FEROCIOUS WILD BEASTS
Will be on Exhibition in the next Block.
MAGNIFICENT FIREWORKS
Were in contemplation for this occasion,
but the idea has been abandoned.
A GRAND TORCHLIGHT PROCESSION
ay be expected; in fact, the public are
ivileged to expect whatever they please.
Doors Open at 7 o'clock
The Trouble to begin at 8 o'clock

We
A GRA
May be
privileg
De
The Tr

At the St. Nicholas hotel N.Y. Papa . . . met mamma, Olivia Louise Langdon. . . .

And papa and mamma were married. Papa wrote mamma a great many beautiful love letters when he was engaged to mamma, but mamma says I am too young to see them yet; I asked papa what I should do for I didn't {know} how I could write a Biography of him without his love-letters, papa said that I could write mamma's oppinion of them, and that would do just as well. So I will do as papa says and mamma says she thinks they are the loveliest love-letters that ever were written. . . . I was born, and my chief occupation then was to cry so I must have added greatly to mamma's care!

As a writer herself, Susy paid close attention to Papa's work routine. She'd seen him write from just after breakfast until just before supper, skipping lunch entirely. On a good day, he filled fifty pages. If he had a sudden stroke of inspiration, neither cold nor dark nor three-in-the-morning kept him from hurrying up to his office to scribble it down.

Papa called it **"sailing right on."**

All too often, however, Papa got . . . well, *distracted.*

He was a famous author, living in the most impressive house in Hartford, Connecticut. Friends, neighbors, and total strangers were eager to spend time with him.

Papa tried to let George, the butler, know when he wasn't interested in receiving visitors.

But sometimes Papa had to suffer when, as he put it, some **"mentally dead people brought their corpses with them for a long visit."**

And then there were the stacks of **"irksome"** letters to answer.

Far too much of Papa's time was used up by being famous!

And so, Papa liked to escape to Quarry Farm in New York, where Mamma's sister lived. He called it **"the quietest of all quiet places,"** far away from peering eyes and pesky visitors.

The animals on the farm *could not care less* that Papa was a world-famous author . . . especially the donkey, Kiditchin, who only gave rides in exchange for treats.

The farm is aunt Susies home and where we stay in the summer, it is situated on the top of a high hill overlooking the valley of Elmira. In the winter papa sent way to Kansas for a little donkey for us to have at the farm, and when we got to the farm we were delighted to find the donky in good trimm and ready to have us ride her. But she has proved to be very balky, and we have to make her go by walking in front of her with a handfull of crackers.

Life on the farm
was so busy, there was
barely time to write!

Our varius occupations are as follows. Papa rises about ½ past 7 in the morning, breakfasts at eight, writes plays tennis with Clara and me . . . tries to make the donkey go in the morning does varius things and in the evening plays tennis with Clara and me and amuses Jean and the donkey. . . .

Clara and I do most every thing from practicing to donkey riding and playing tag. While Jean's time is spent in asking mamma what she can have to eat. . . .

There are eleven cats at the farm here now. . . .

It is very {funny} to see what papa calls the cat prosession it was formed in this way. Old Minnie-cat headed (the mother of all the cats), next to her came aunt Susie, then Clara on the donkey, accompanied by a file of cats, then papa and Jean hand in hand and a file of cats brought up the rear, mamma and I made up the audience.

But despite their busy schedules, Papa and Susy did find time to write.

Susy carefully copied samples of Papa's work into the biography: essays he wrote about Civil War hero Ulysses S. Grant, and a little poem he composed in honor of the donkey, Kiditchin.

O you dear Kiditchin
You are totally bewitchin:
"Waw - - - he!"
Our summer days Kiditchin
Thour't dear from nose to britchin
"Waw - - - he!"....
Anon lift up thy song—
Thy noble note prolong—....
"Waw - - - he! Waw - - - he! Waw - - - he!"
Swetest donkey man ever saw.

STEP SOFTLY!
KEEP AWAY!
DO NOT DISTURB
THE REMAINS!

Papa wrote in a special octagonal study Aunt Susie had built for him. On hot days, he opened all the windows and then **"anchored"** his papers with brickbats so they wouldn't fly away. There, he worked on books such as *Adventures of Huckleberry Finn*, which Papa called a **"rattling good"** novel about a runaway boy who helps a slave escape down the Mississippi River.

He wrote all day and read the pages to the family at night.

Susy recounted how Papa then relied on Mamma's good taste to clean up any questionable passages.

Papa read "Hucleberry Finn" to us in manuscript . . . and then he would leave parts of it with mamma to expergate . . . and I remember so well, with what pangs of regret we used to see her turn down the leaves of the pages which meant, that some delightfully dreadful part must be scratched out.

Susy herself had definite opinions about Papa's work. She loved *The Prince and the Pauper* for its "lovely, charming ideas" and beautiful language. Susy saw Papa's "kind, sympathetic nature" as they "promenaded up and down the library" every evening, discussing, as Papa put it, **"affairs of State, or the deep questions of human life, or our small personal affairs."**

He is known to the public as a humorist, but he has much more in him that is earnest than that is humorous. . .

Papa can make exceedingly bright jokes, and he enjoys funny things, and when he is with people he jokes and laughs a great deal, but . . . when we are all alone at home nine times

out of ten, he talks about some very
earnest subject . . . ; he doesn't joke
as much, tell many more funny stories
than most men. . . .

He is as much a Pholosopher as
any thing I think.

The months passed as Susy detailed her observations of Papa to present a well-rounded picture. She wrote of things serious — since Papa was sometimes serious — such as his efforts to establish an international copyright law and his painstaking work publishing Grant's memoirs.

And she wrote of things silly — since Papa was sometimes silly.

The other day we were all sitting when papa told Clara and I that he would give us an arithmetic example. . . . "If _A_ byes a horse for $200 and _B_ byes a mule for $140 and they join in copartnership and trade their chreatures for a piece of land $480 how long will it take a . . . man to borrow a silk umbrella.

MARK
TWAIN
THE ADVENTURES OF
TOM SAWYER

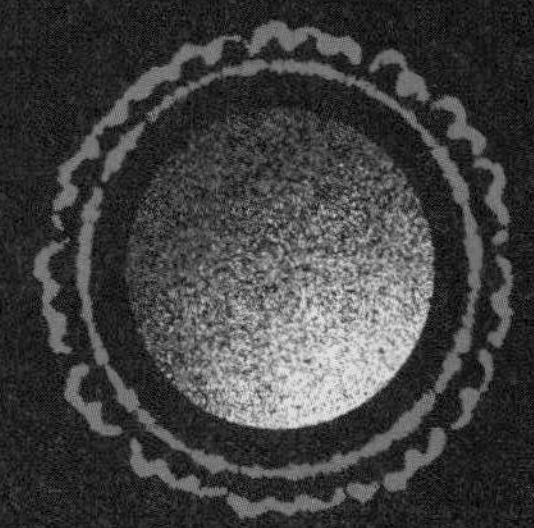

Like Papa, Susy wrote and wrote, filling over 130 pages.

To conclude her biography, she relied on an eyewitness account to provide an anecdote that summed up Papa perfectly.

The other day, mamma went into the library and found papa sitting there reading a book, and roaring with laughter over it; she asked him what he was reading, he answered that he hadn't stopped to look at the title of the book . . . she glanced over his shoulder at the cover, and found it was one of his own books.

Papa approved wholeheartedly.

Susy had been a **"kindly biographer,"** to be sure. **"Yet to a quite creditable degree,"** he decided, she was also **"loyal to the responsibilities of her position as historian"** and gave him **"a quiet prod now and then."**

Her observations were so **"clear and nicely shaded"** that twenty years later, when he published his autobiography, he included his favorite passages from Susy's notebook.

And so, people finally got just what Susy thought they needed: a portrait of the funny, serious, absentminded, cat-loving, billiard-playing, philosophical Papa — the extraordinary Mark Twain, according to Susy.

AUTHOR'S NOTE

Papa

"He has a keen sense of the ludicrous, notices funny stories and incidents, knows how to tell them, to improve upon them, and does not forget them. . . . But still he is more interested in earnest books and earnest subjects."
— Susy Clemens

Samuel Clemens was "Papa" to his daughter Susy, but most of the world knew him by his pen name, "Mark Twain." He remains one of the best-known and most beloved of all American authors. Even people who have not read his books know his name and likely could pick his photo out of a lineup.

He is probably most famous for two novels. *The Adventures of Tom Sawyer* relates the summer escapades of Tom Sawyer and his best friend, Huckleberry Finn. *Adventures of Huckleberry Finn*, widely regarded as Twain's masterpiece, tells how Huck makes the heroic decision to help a slave named Jim escape from his owner. Twain broke new ground by writing *Huckleberry Finn* in the vernacular, using dialects of a specific locality — becoming the first major American novelist to do so. The novel begins, "You don't know about me without you have read a book by the name of *The Adventures of Tom Sawyer*; but that ain't no matter. That book was made by Mr. Mark Twain, and he told the truth, mainly. There was things which he stretched, but mainly he told the truth."

When it was first published, a few critics praised *Adventures of Huckleberry Finn* as truthful and realistic, but most critics did not agree. They thought the book was coarse in language and content. "If Mr. Clemens cannot think of something better to tell our pure-minded lads and lasses," declared Louisa May Alcott, author of *Little Women*, "he had best stop writing for them." The book was also banned by the library committee of Concord, Massachusetts.

Over time, however, the novel has come to be seen as a masterpiece. Ernest Hemingway said that "all modern American literature comes from . . . *Huckleberry Finn*. . . . It's the best book we've had."

Twain's work is still read and discussed and admired a hundred years after his death because of his utterly original sense of humor and his keen insights into the American character.

Susy

"I think a great deal of her work. . . . I feel that my own portrait, with some of the defects fined down and others left out, is here. . . . Little creature though Susy was, the penetration which was born in her finds its way to the surface more than once in these pages."
— Mark Twain

I'd been considering writing a book about Twain for years when, in 2007, I stumbled across an interesting historical footnote: his thirteen-year-old daughter, Susy, wrote a biography of him.

I was immediately intrigued. I knew that a biography by any member of his family would be intimate and revealing. But I was especially curious because, having been the parent of a thirteen-year-old girl myself, I know they tend to call it like they see it.

Susy did not disappoint me.

From the spring of 1885 until the summer of 1886, she worked on the biography. The little brown notebook also served as a diary of sorts. In addition to her observations of Twain, she also recorded personal, day-to-day events. In fact, it was during the recording of a diary entry that the notebook ends. After her final biographical entry — the telling anecdote of Twain laughing uproariously over one of his own books — Susy wrote in the notebook only twice more. On June 26, 1886, she noted the route the family planned to take to visit Grandma Clemens in Keokuk, Iowa; a few days later, Susy wrote, "July 4. We have arrived in Keokuk after a very pleasant" —

The notebook ends here. It's interesting to speculate what might have pulled her away from her writing, mid-sentence. A family meal? A Fourth of July celebration? According to Twain, Susy's "days became increasingly busy with studies and work, and she never resumed the biography." Still, it remains an intimate portrait of Mark Twain by someone who knew and loved him best.

For the rest of Twain's life, he treasured the biography, misspellings and all — even more so after Susy's tragic death in 1896 from spinal meningitis, at the age of twenty-four. By this time, Twain had already suffered two terrible losses: his younger brother, Henry, who died in 1858 in a steamboat accident; and a son, Langdon, who died at age two from diphtheria, about two months after Susy was born. The loss of Susy, however, may have been the hardest for Twain to bear. After her death, he wrote to a friend, "I did not know that she could go away and take our lives with her, yet leave our dull bodies behind. . . . My fortune is gone, I am a pauper."

Knowing that "the hand that traced" the final line was gone forever made the biography all the more valuable in Twain's eyes. In his autobiography, he wrote, "I have had no compliment, no praise, no tribute from any source, that was so precious to me as this one was and still is. As I read it *now*, after all these many years, it is still a king's message to me."

Ten years after Susy's death, Twain published "Chapters from My Autobiography" in the literary magazine *North American Review* from September 1906 until December 1907. In an October 1906 issue, he introduced his "busy bee." For the next thirteen months, readers were treated to a revealing portrait of one of America's most beloved authors — the extraordinary Mark Twain, according to Susy.

The biography now resides in the Albert and Shirley Small Special Collections at the University of Virginia Library. It was also published in 1985 as the book *Papa: An Intimate Biography of Mark Twain*, edited by Charles Neider.

WRITING AN EXTRAORDINARY BIOGRAPHY

(According to Barbara Kerley)*

You can write a biography, too. Why not start with a member of your family, like Susy did? Just follow her lead. . . .

First, she gathered information on her subject — in this case, Papa.

Susy observed Papa carefully to learn:

- his physical appearance
- his personality
- his routines and habits
- his likes and dislikes

Tip: You can study your subject through personal observation or by reading the accounts of others. Be sure to take good notes so that you won't forget anything important.

She gathered additional information by:

- conducting interviews
- reading books, articles, and letters

Tip: Whenever possible, use primary sources — things written by people who actually know or knew your subject. Think of primary sources as eyewitness accounts.

Next, she started writing. Susy worked hard to make sure her biography was accurate, being, as Papa put it, "loyal to her position as historian." So she was careful to get the facts straight:

- people
- places
- dates
- events
- quotations

Tip: Always double check your facts. (This is when you'll be really glad you took good notes!)

Susy wanted her readers to get to know the "real" Mark Twain. She brought her portrait to life by including:

- specific details
- lots of examples
- interesting quotations

Tip: Writers follow the rule "Show, don't tell." To make your biography lively, instead of just telling your readers that your subject is funny, give them an example of one of your subject's jokes.

Susy created a well-rounded portrait of Papa by showing:

- his fine and not-so-fine habits
- his serious and silly sides
- his difficulties as a child and his successes as an adult

Tip: Everyone has flaws and everyone struggles from time to time, even famous people who have done great things. Providing a balanced account will help your readers see your subject as a real person.

Finally, Susy asked for writing advice when she needed it. Susy consulted with a fellow author (in this case, Papa!).

Tip: Even if you don't happen to live with a world-famous author, you can get writing help from a teacher, parent, or librarian. There are lots of people eager to see you write your own, extraordinary biography.

**with a lot of help from Susy*

For a printable page, go to: www.Barbarakerley.com/teachers.html

A SELECTED TIME LINE OF MARK TWAIN'S LIFE

1835 — born Samuel Langhorne Clemens on November 30 in Florida, Missouri

1839 — moves to Hannibal, Missouri, the model for the setting of his future novels *The Adventures of Tom Sawyer* and *Adventures of Huckleberry Finn*

1847 — begins working as an apprentice at his first newspaper job, at the *Hannibal Gazette*

1848–1861 — works as a printer, writer, editor, steamboat pilot on the Mississippi River, and silver prospector

1863 — adopts the pen name "Mark Twain," a steamboat term signifying safe water twelve feet deep

1865 — publishes the story that makes him famous across America, "Jim Smiley and His Jumping Frog"

1869 — *The Innocents Abroad*

1870 — marries Olivia Langdon

1872 — Susy Clemens born; *Roughing It*

1874 — Clara Clemens born; moves into his home in Hartford, Connecticut, and embarks on the most productive time in his career

1876 — *The Adventures of Tom Sawyer*

1880 — Jean Clemens born

1881 — *The Prince and the Pauper*

1883 — *Life on the Mississippi*

1885 — *Adventures of Huckleberry Finn*

1889 — *A Connecticut Yankee in King Arthur's Court*

1891 — due to financial difficulties, closes down the Hartford house and takes his family to Europe

1908 — moves into final home in Redding, Connecticut

1910 — dies on April 21 in Redding, Connecticut, and is buried in Elmira, New York

The text type was set in Adobe Garamond Pro, Clarendon BT Bold Condensed, and Mona Lisa Solid ITC. The journal type was set in LinotypeZapfino One.
The illustrations were done in digital media.
Front and back cover design by Edwin Fotheringham.
Art direction and book design by Marijka Kostiw.

ISBN-13: 978-0-545-34127-1
ISBN-10: 0-545-34127-2

6 7 8 9 10 40 20 19 18 17 16 15

PHOTO COURTESY OF THE MARK TWAIN HOUSE & MUSEUM, HARTFORD, CT.

From left to right: Clara, Mama, Jean, Papa, Susy and their dog, Hash.

ACKNOWLEDGMENTS
A microfilm of the entire manuscript of Susy Clemens's biography of her father, together with notes and comments by Mark Twain, was made available through the courtesy of the Albert and Shirley Small Special Collections, University of Virginia Library.
Special thanks to: Laura Skandera Trombley of Pitzer College for fact checking the book; Margaret Hrabe and Greg Johnson of the Albert and Shirley Small Special Collections, University of Virginia Library; Rey Antonio of the University of Virginia Printing & Copying Services; and Matthew Miles of the Humboldt County Library, California

For Baba—with thanks—BK *As always, for my extraordinary wife and kids—EF*

SOURCES

All excerpts from Susy's biography, including handwritten notes inserted by Mark Twain, were drawn from the original manuscript, housed in the Albert and Shirley Small Special Collections at the University of Virginia Library. For the convenience of readers who do not have access to the University of Virginia Library, an additional source from the book *Papa* is also listed below. Quotations in the text were drawn from the following sources:

Pages 2–3 "This is a frank . . .": Mark Twain, "Chapters From My Autobiography," *North American Review* (hereafter *NAR*), October 19, 1906, Vol. 183: No. 6, p. 711.

6–7 "annoyed": *Biography of Mark Twain*, Albert and Shirley Small Special Collections, University of Virginia Library, 5; hereafter *Biography*; also found in Susy Clemens, *Papa: An Intimate Biography of Mark Twain*, ed. Charles Neider (Garden City, NY: Doubleday, 1985), 106; hereafter *Papa.*

8–9 "It troubles me . . .": *Biography*, 5; also found in *Papa*, 106.
"I never saw . . .": *Biography*, 6; also found in *Papa*, 107.
"the busiest bee . . .": *NAR* Oct 19, 1906, 183:6, p. 705.
"We are a very . . .": *Biography*, 1; also found in *Papa*, 83–84.

12–13 "He does tell . . .": *Biography*, 2; also found in *Papa*, 84.
"He has a peculiar gait…": *Biography*, 3; also found in *Papa*, 99.
"His favorite game is…": *Biography*, 2; also found in *Papa*, 89.
"He has got a temper…": *Biography*, 1; also found in *Papa*, 84.
"He is…oh…": *Biography*, 2; also found in *Papa*, 84.
"He smokes…": *Biography*, 2; also found in *Papa*, 89.
"Papa uses…": *Biography*, 4; also found in *Papa*, 100.

14–15 "deep pleasure": *NAR* Oct 19, 1906, 183:6, pp. 705–706.
"frequently desperate": *NAR* Oct 19, 1906, 183:6, p. 706.
"cover up . . .": *NAR* Oct 19, 1906, 183:6, p. 716.
"secretly and . . .": *NAR* Oct 19, 1906, 183:6, p. 705.

16–17 "Papa said the other day . . .": *Biography*, 4–5; also found in *Papa*, 101.

18–19 "Papa was born . . .": *Biography*, 7–8; also found in *Papa*, 110–111, 112.

20–21 handbill: http://www.pbs.org/marktwain/scrapbook/04_trouble/index.html
"At the St. Nicholas . . .": *Biography*, 9–12; also found in *Papa*, 113–117.

22–23 "sailing right on": Henry Nash Smith and William M. Gibson, eds., *Mark Twain—Howells Letters*, (Cambridge, MA: The Belknap Press of Harvard University Press, 1960), 435.

24–25 "mentally dead people . . .": Clara Clemens, *My Father, Mark Twain* (New York: Harper & Brothers, 1931), 42.
"irksome": Dixon Wecter, ed., *Mark Twain to Mrs. Fairbanks*, (San Marino, CA: Huntington Library, 1949), 232.

26–27 "the quietest . . .": Edith Colgate Salsbury, ed., *Susy and Mark Twain: Family Dialogues*, (New York: Harper & Row, 1965), 53.
"The farm is . . .": *Biography*, 40; also found in *Papa*, 142–144.

28–29 "Our varius occupations . . .": *Biography*, 42–44; also found in *Papa*, 146–147.
"There are eleven cats…": *Biography*, 42; also found in *Papa*, 145–146.

30–31 "O you dear . . .": *Papa*, 144–145.

32–33 "anchored": Albert Bigelow Paine, ed., *Mark Twain's Letters* (New York: Harper & Brothers, 1917), 1:225.
"rattling good": Justin Kaplan, *Mr. Clemens and Mark Twain*, (New York: Simon & Shuster, 1966), 251; hereafter *Mr. Clemens.*

34–35 "Papa read 'Hucleberry Finn' . . .": *Biography*, 87–88; also found in *Papa*, 188–189.

36–37 "lovely charming ideas": *Biography*, 5; also found in *Papa*, 107.
"kind sympathetic nature": *Biography*, 5; also found in *Papa*, 107.
"promenaded up and down . . .": *Biography*, 86; also found in *Papa*, 187.
"affairs of State . . .": *NAR* Aug 2, 1907, 185:7, p. 691.
"He is known . . .": *Biography*, 108–110; also found in *Papa*, 206–207.

38–39 "The other day we were . . . Papa told Clara . . .": *Biography*, 39; also found in *Papa*, 140–142.

40–41 "The other day mamma went . . .": *Biography*, 130; also found in *Papa*, 225.

42–43 "kindly biographer": *NAR* May 17, 1907, 185:2, p. 117.
"Yet to a quite . . .": *NAR* May 17, 1907, 185:2, p. 117.
"clear and nicely shaded": *NAR* May 17, 1907, 185:2, p. 117.

Quotations in the Author's Note were drawn from the following sources:

"He has a keen . . .": *Biography*, 108–109; also found in *Papa*, 206–207.
"You don't know . . .": Mark Twain, *Adventures of Huckleberry Finn* (New York: Harper & Brothers, 1912)
"If Mr. Clemens . . .": *Mr. Clemens*, 268.
"all modern American . . .": R. Kent Rasmussen, *Mark Twain A to Z* (New York: Facts on File, 1995), 217.
"I think a great deal . . .": *NAR* May 17, 1907, 185:2, p. 117.
"July 4. We have arrived . . .": *Biography*, 131; also found in *Papa*, 225.
"days became increasingly . . .": notation written by Mark Twain in the *Biography*; also found in *Papa*, 229.
"I did not know . . .": Charles Neider, ed., *The Selected Letters of Mark Twain* (New York: Harper & Row, 1982), 242.
"the hand that traced": notation written by Mark Twain in the *Biography*; also found in *Papa*, 229.
"I have had no compliment . . .": *NAR* Oct 19, 1906, 183:6, p. 706.
"busy bee": *NAR* 20 Oct 19, 1906, 183:6, p. 705.